Major Walker

Militiana, and other rhymes

Major Walker

Militiana, and other rhymes

ISBN/EAN: 9783337261214

Printed in Europe, USA, Canada, Australia, Japan

Cover: Foto ©Thomas Meinert / pixelio.de

More available books at **www.hansebooks.com**

MILITIANA,

AND OTHER RHYMES.

BY

MAJOR WALKER, WEST YORK RIFLES,

(*A " Disembodied" Spirit.*)

"Militia est potior."—*Hor.* lib. i. sat. 1.

LONDON:
WYMAN & SONS, GREAT QUEEN STREET,
LINCOLN'S-INN FIELDS, W.C.
1873.

CONTENTS.

MILITIANA.

	PAGE
At Edinburgh	1
At Aldershot.—South Camp	4
At Hythe	7
At Dover	10
At Woolmer	13
At Cahir	15
At Aldershot.—North Camp	18
At Shorncliffe	20
At Cashel	22
At Ayr	25
The Training	26
Our Regimental Races	29
The Field Day	32
The Sergeant-major	35
The School for the Reserve	37
The Autumn of 1872	40
A Captain's Plea	42
The Orderly Officer's Report	43

CONTENTS.

WAR LYRICS.

(A.D. 1870.)

	PAGE
"To Arms!"	47
Good Taste (?)	49
An Awkward Age	50
"'The Times'" Surrender	51
"To Rifle, Rob, and Plunder!"	53
Thorwaldsen's Lion	54
German Resolve	55
Hark, Bismarck!	55
Lutetia, December, 1870	56
"Militia est Potior"	57
Absit Omen!	60

―――o―――

MISCELLANEA.

Valentines	64, 94
Charades	66, 69, 70, 84, 91, 93, 98
Acrostics	67, 101, 107
Epigrams	84, 104, 105
An Eclogue	109
Spring	113
Friendship	115
Exodus	117

&c. &c. &c.

MILITIANA.

AT EDINBURGH.

THE gallant Rifles gave a ball;
Our martinet old General,
So Argus-eyed, on faults would fall,
    As sure as Armstrong gun.
An Ensign was detail'd for guard,
Lamenting that he was debarr'd
    From joining in the fun.

But what won't ladies' charms achieve?—
His conduct to record I grieve,
    Yet Truth must have her say:
That Ensign, 'mid the glittering throng,
Was seen that night the sylphs among—
    The gayest of the gay!

The revelry was at its height,
In the small hours of the night,
When, lo! he saw a moving sight—
 The Cock'd Hat going away!
Oh! now the truth he'll surely learn—
For well our Ensign knew he'd turn
 The Guard out on his way.

No time to think! He left the room,
Sprang up behind the great man's brougham,
And as, beneath the grateful gloom,
 They near'd the castle-gate,
Rush'd from his perch, turn'd out his men,
Open'd the ranks, fix'd swords, and then
 The Grand Rounds did await.

In great amaze, the K.C.B.
Stared at our hero as if he
 Possess'd a Gorgon's head.
"Sir, you were at the Ball to-night!"
But not a word, save "Guard all right!"
 That prudent Ensign said.

"Were you, or weren't you, at the Ball?"
"The Guard's all right, sir!" that was all
 This parrot would avouch.
A madder, but no wiser man,
The Gen'ral left the barbican,
Swearing, "I'll break him if I can!"
 And sought his knightly couch.

AT ALDERSHOT.—SOUTH CAMP.

It's quite a feat to find your room,
When, 'mongst the huts, in midnight gloom
You see each block before you loom,
    Exactly like another;
If e'er it be your luck to make
The trial, I could dare to stake
All GUNTER'S to a penny cake,
    You'll say at least, "Oh, bother!"

So fared the gallant Major R——,
As, with contemplative cigar,
He sought his quarters near and far,

With very ill success;
Although—or p'raps you'll say, because—
He'd dined full well, his vision was
    Still rather in a " mess " !

The sentries challenged him no end,
Although F. O., he answer'd, " Friend."
    —" Ah, here's the door at last ! "
So in he rush'd. Whom did he see,
But newly-married Colonel B——,
A stately form in *robe de nuit*,
    At which he stood aghast !

" I think, sir, this is going too far ! "
" Beg pardon, sir, I'm Major R——."
" I don't care who the deuce you are,
    Here you can have no right ! "
The Major, seeing 'twas in vain,
Choked back his efforts to explain,
Emerged into the gloom again,
    And never said " Good night ! '

This thought no doubt then soothed his mind:
'Tis not unusual to find
    A Colonel in an 'ut;
Join'd with a wish, not loud but deep,
That Colonels would in future keep—
Especially when going to sleep—
    Their doors more closely shut!

AT HYTHE.

I SING of Hythe in heathen days,
Ere from the error of their ways
Poor SNIDER, for less pay than praise,
    Our Enfields had converted.
A great invention—that the boon
Was not conferr'd a day too soon
    May safely be asserted!

There, on the beach, the squads were taught
To use the rifle as they ought,
Which *then* they to the "order" brought,
    And through the muzzle fed it.

But ramrods *now* we only use
To shoot spectators at reviews—
An art the sooner we can lose
    The better for our credit.*

Though target-practice seem'd a bore
To elbows stiff and shoulders sore,
Position-drill was something more.
    At first it made you stare :
" No movement of 'ead, harm, or heye,
Restrain your breathing, don't aim 'igh,
Now squeeze the trigger quietly !
    How simple !—As you were ! "

A Course of Musketry, in sooth,
Like true love, never did run smooth :
First-class Certificates can't soothe
    Beyond a certain measure.

---

   * This was written in 1869, before the Reserve Forces were armed with breech-loaders.

A double o'er the s(h)ingle too,
To catch your papers as they flew,
Blown by the wind a mile or two,
    Was anything but pleasure.

But *désagréments*, great and small,
Were gladly borne by one and all,
For by such means alone we shall
    Keep England's flag unfurl'd.
Then long may Hythe, with weapons true,
Train Musketry Instructors, who
Will make our Army through and through
    The marksmen of the world!

AT DOVER.

Ours was a hunting regiment,
And lots of sport we had in Kent,
A country where, if there's a scent,
    The hounds are safe to kill;
But whether you can see it all,
Unless you've a horse that *cannot* fall,
Is doubtful, and the odds are small
    I'd lay against a spill.

Stone walls are awkward things, I wist,
But wire fences are awkwardest,
And *why offences* like these exist,
    Is a fact I can't explain.

Your horse can't see, and won't rise at them, hence
You must sing the lines that, I think, commence—
"*I'll hang my coat on the wire fence,
And I'll go at the jump again!*"

Now, such a NIMROD was our chief,
He never yet, 'tis my belief,
    Refused one leave for hunting;
But, if you wish'd your friends to see,
To visit local scenery,
Or to attend a pic-nic, he
    Would no doubt send you shunting!

The orderly officer, once, they say,
Determined not to lose a day,
Had order'd round his gallant grey,
    And, to avoid dispute, he
Inspected rations in tops and spurs!
As he said to his brother officers,
"What else can you do if the Meet occurs
    The day you're down for duty?"

In France, far other is the case—
There, sporting Captains join the chase,
Blazing with medals and gold lace;
 Indeed, it has been stated,
That Reynard often meets his doom
Slain by a warrior's sword thrust home,
 The hounds being blown or sated!
This tale, however, I am glad,
In justice to Mossoo, to add,
 Is not authenticated!

AT WOOLMER.

A FLYING column's weary feet,
Through eighteen miles of dust and heat,
Where Surrey's fields and Hampshire meet,
    To Woolmer bent their way.
No kite or vulture caught a whiff
Of slaughter imminent; so if
Such birds were near, from sullen cliff
They watch'd the march of our "magnif-
    icently stern array."

We pitch'd our tents in soaking rain:
Next day the hill that flank'd the plain
Re-echoed loud to many a strain,
    From trumpet, fife, and drum.
The votaries of husbandry
Flock'd open-mouth'd in crowds to see;
Through all the day, unceasingly,
    The cry was still—They come!

The ignorance of some of these
Untravell'd aborigines, [freeze,
In SHAKSPEARE'S words, "your blood would
    And harrow up your soul."
How would the learnèd FORSTER groan,
To hear a stalwart rustic own
He'd never heard the name or known,
F. M. the DUKE OF WELLINGTON,
    Or left his native knoll!

And still, no doubt, the bumpkins tell,
How that an army terrible
Invaded once their peaceful dell,
    And camp'd upon the spot;
Then, having spent a summer's day,
Like gipsies, disappear'd away,
Whither, they know not,—others say
    To distant Aldershot.

AT CAHIR.

Our rear division, Number Ten,*
Own'd as commander, Captain N.,
Who, M.F.H. at present, then
   Was Master of the Hawks.
How temperate he was you'd know,
If to his rooms you chanced to go,
And saw his bell-pulls made of So-
   da-water-bottle-Corks.

Let but the day be fresh and clear,
Parade being over, never fear,
With shouts of beaters you would hear
   Each copse and meadow ring.
His war-cry was, "Hoo! ha! ha! ha!"
Which told the country near and far,
   The hawk was on the wing.

---

* Companies were at that time termed "divisions."

Then came the "field"—the mounted few
O'er hedge and ditch careering flew,
While jolly "subs" on foot broke through—
   Unlicensed hawkers they!
Were pigeons strong, and good the pace,
The field were oft in evil case
And distanced, for sometimes the chase
   Would finish miles away.

Once a blue-rock of gallant breed,
A bird of more than wonted speed,
Got clean away—the hawk, thus freed,
   Cared not for voice nor lure,
But spread his wings the skies to cross;
Poor N. bewail'd his fav'rite's loss—
The best bird on the cadge he was,
   None else of blood so pure.

For weeks and months, on wall and tree,
" LOST " in big letters seen might be,

But of his darling's welfare he
   No tidings heard. Poor buffer!
He look'd distracted—all could see
   What pangs he had to suffer ;
Till in the neighb'ring town he spies
His long-lost hawk, with glassy eyes,
Staring at him in mute surprise,
And o'er the window, " Mr. Vyse,
   Bird-fancier and Stuffer ! "

AT ALDERSHOT.—NORTH CAMP.

Who that has lain at Aldershot
(And what old Army man has not?)
Says, 46th like, "*I've forgot
    Those field days of renown,*"
When, from his seat in grey Whitehall,
With notice scant, or none at all,
    The Royal GEORGE came down?

Then officers of every grade,
But chiefly majors of brigade,
    Went pricking o'er the ground;
Despatches seeing, Colonels guess,
"O.H.M.S.—Oh, here's a mess!
They've hardly left us time to dress,
    Go, bid the bugles sound!"

Then the Long Valley—What's the word?—
To call it dusty were absurd,
    The richest language fails;
We'll try a negative instead;
There's "none so dusty," may be said,
    'Mong all our English vales.

But dust might whelm, or rain might fall,
By Cæsar's Camp or wide canal,
    Forth march'd our *corps d'armée*,
As 'fore this star of English peers,
At Inkerman, the Grenadiers,
Or Dover's heights the Volunteers,
    Upon a recent day.

Though thus undoubtedly a swell,
That CAMBRIDGE rules the Army well
    All but a few confess;
'Twas he increased the soldier's pay,
And, now "the cat" is chased away:
Health to the Royal Duke, and may
    His shadow ne'er grow less!

AT SHORNCLIFFE.

A SOUTHERN camp o'erlooks the sea,
And all who know it will agree,
For mirth and gay society,
  It well deserves a song.
One day the lines were all alive,
Watching a regiment arrive,
Which to the tune of "Ninety-five"
  Came gallantly along.

Meanwhile, in lady's bower so rare,
Sat one of sixteen Nieces fair,
  On pen and ink intent,
Inditing, from her Aunt's dictation,
Sweet little notes of invitation
  For the new regiment.

"And mark, my dear," her Aunt pursued,
As Army List in hand she stood,
" Our rooms are small, so where's the good
  Of asking nobodies?
This well-read list their titles tells,
The baronets and honourables,
The lords and other dear young swells—
  We'll send invites to these."

But such the *esprit* of that *corps*,
That when the interval pass'd o'er,
The favour'd ones would come no more
  Than those who'd been neglected :
And if, in thinking on their loss,
The Nieces look'd a wee bit cross,
Their friends remark'd it only was
  What they might have expected!

AT CASHEL.

NONE but a cold misogynist,
As each name in the *Army List*
Will frankly own, could long resist
   The charms of Erin's daughters.
Though War's sad losses we deplore,
Our mess-tables have suffer'd more
By Love's besieging' o'er and o'er,
On that too-hospitable shore,
   Across St. George's waters.

The wit that can each charm enhance,
The step unrivall'd in the dance,
The haughty and yet melting glance,
   To you so sweetly partial,

A glamour cast that makes you blest,
And heedless of to-morrow's quest,
The reprimand, the close arrest,
    And haply, the court-martial.

Your host, perchance, is just as bad,
Though brave and pure as Galahad,
Well skill'd to keep his table glad,
    And thoughtful to amuse you;
But, let his kindness have its course,
He'd cut your traces, hide your horse,
Detain you by coercion's force,
    Sooner than he should lose you.

Then at the ball in barracks, where
The pretty ones look twice as fair,
Half wondering how they could dare
    To cross such naughty portals!
Till, as their hands their partners claim,
They find, despite their rakish name,
Wild red-coats can be quite as tame
    As ordinary mortals.

Yes! English husbands, Irish wives—
This is the plan which Fate contrives
To give some Britons happy lives;
   But, Benedicts, I warn ye,
Lest at the outset you should fail
To please, forget not ere you sail—
Ere yet the bridal blush be pale—
   To take them to Killarney!

AT AYR.

A CAPTAIN, rather past his work,
His duty daily tried to shirk,
  To our extreme vexation;
In wiser ranks, at any rate,
He would have been a candidate
  For superannuation.

If for a " board " detailed was he,
Or for " fatigue " or " orderly,"
  Or at the butts to shoot, he
Searching for substitutes began,
Till through our lines the saying ran,
" *Thompson expects some other man*
  Each day will do his duty ! "

THE TRAINING.

"Each bullet has its billet," says
A well-used saw of warlike days,
And one which cuts in divers ways,
    According as you pull it;
If thus we might the system quell,
And do away with it pell-mell,
Then, Mr. CARDWELL, 't were as well
    Each billet had its bullet!

How can we of our wisdom boast,
When, for a regimental post,
We choose the spot that has the most
    Pot-houses in the county?

No use to " cry the credit down,"
The landlords know throughout the town
Each man will soon have, all his own,
    At least a pound of bounty.

No sight can well be more absurd,
" Parade in billets " being the word,
If thunder's warning has been heard,
    Or clouds seem bent on raining ;
In stuffy rooms the squads are found,
Bed-posts, not out-posts, rallying round,
Up creaking stairs pay-sergeants pound,
    The martyrs of the training.

If you, to check that grievous sin—
Absence from quarters—would begin,
No barrack-gates to keep them in,
    Nor sentries to restrain ;
Truant recruits, with lawless aims,
At tattoo answer to their names,
And on their little varied games
    Soon sally forth again.

But vain, I fear, to make them known ;
Our wrongs the country ne'er will own,
Whilst on one side our swords are thrown,
    To rust unused, inactive ;
But should stern War unsheath the blade,
Our rulers then may wish that they'd—
E'en with an adverse Budget—made
    The Service more attractive.

OUR REGIMENTAL RACES.

THE hunting season barely past,
His head each horse was eating fast,
A state of things which could not last
      On bonny Yorkshire's plains ;
Where, if it's known a horse can go,
He'll not be long kept up for show ;
But to provide him worthy foe
      Are spared nor purse nor pains.

This tells at once why now we see
A gay and gallant company
Assembled round our T. Y. C.
      And crowning the Grand Stand :

While by the flag six hunting cracks,
All with their owners on their backs,
And each well-known to neighbouring packs,
    Await the starter's wand.

They're off. Swift Kamtoplokamos
And Grub exert their utmost force
To prove which is the better horse:
    While close behind them, rushing,
Comes Priam—first at many goals—
Who swerves against the hurdle-poles,
And on his rider falls and rolls,
    His leg beneath him crushing.

More hurdles, then they reach the brook;
One, two, three, four have cross'd it. Look!
The fifth refuses—'tis the Duke;
    And "Murska wins," they cry.
Then, pelting hotly up the hill,
Murska, the favourite, leading still,
With Felstan close upon her heel,
    And ridden splendidly.

But "who laughs last he laughs the most,"
For Murska went wrong side the post,
And Felstan won. The shouting host
    Might have been heard at Varna.
Other events 'twere long to tell;
But, being all contested well,
Their record will be found in *Bell*,
    Though not *Militiana*.

THE FIELD DAY.

(A Souvenir of Aldershot.)

ALL ceaselessly along the wold
The tide of mimic war had roll'd,
And now our scatter'd ranks were told
  To close and form brigades.
The Royal Standard floated high
O'er England's Monarch dashing by,
Surrounded by her chivalry
  And proudly mounted *aides*.

The skirmishers in many a chain,
Or dotted singly o'er the plain,
Now doubled in with might and main,
  Responsive to the call—

Which bugles sang with loud acclaim—
While glittering-belted rifles came,
And linesmen with their coats of flame,
  And bear-skinn'd guardsmen tall.

The marching-past may now requite
Our toils; for, girt with heroes bright,
Our lady beams upon our sight
  The brightest of them all.

The "Household" first, the "Heavies" then,
The Lancers and Hussars—the men
Who charged the guns as one to ten
  On Balaclava's field;
Then the far-famed Artillery,
And then the British Infantry,
First on the scroll of Victory,
  To none their claims may yield.

The bands combined our ears astound
With splendid bursts of martial sound,
As, with a tread that shakes the ground,
  The gallant troops go by;

When the saluting post it nears
Each regiment its quick-step hears,
Familiar as the badge it bears,
 And wide the colours fly.

Then gladly to our lines we wend.—
Far be the day when field-days end,
And War's realities descend
 On peaceful hill and dale ;
And long may men behold their Queen,
Though by her side no more is seen
Her Consort, clad in rifle-green,
 The garb he loved so well.

THE SERGEANT-MAJOR.

The Colonel's voice dispenses doom
To culprits in the orderly-room ;
    But equally or more
The Sergeant-major wields a sway
Which Sergeants tremble and obey,
    And Corporals adore.

No rifle chafes his gallant hands,
Begirt with sword erect he stands,
    And spurns with martial heel
The clanking scabbard, while he shows
The crude recruitlings how to close,
    To countermarch and wheel.

In regiments of a thousand men,
Though Captains you may count by ten,
    Subalterns by the score,
Though stripes and chevrons throng the
    ground,
There's but *one* Sergeant-major found,
    You'll ne'er discover more.

Then mark him at the column's head,
While "*Scots wha hae wi' Wallace bled*"
    Clangs forth from trump and drum,
And in his firm step you shall see
Smartness, which, if the Fates agree,
Shall through the ranks reflected be,
    And strike detraction dumb.

THE SCHOOL FOR THE RESERVE.

WE love to thoughts of peace to cling,
But must, late wars remembering,
Of infant schools not only sing
    But schools of infantry ;
Where officers strain every nerve
To form themselves, with zeal and *verve*,
The nucleus of the great Reserve
    Which England pants to see.

Here York and Lancaster are not
At daggers drawn ; the canny Scot
Seeks only—Bannockburn forgot—
    The Southron's praise to win ;

With wit as trenchant as their blades
Come officers, of varied grades,
From where the classic verdure shades
    The Fields of Lincoln's Inn.

First mimicking the awkward pace
Of the famed bird of Michaelmas,
Whose image now usurps the place
    Of partridge and of pheasant,
While,—if the Tennysonian Muse
This little freedom will excuse,—
" *The shingle grinding 'neath the*"—shoes
    Feels the reverse of pleasant.

Then, step by step advancing, till
As sergeants, privates, what you will,
From front to rear all know their drill,
    By slow and sure degrees;
Now quite prepared to do the grand,
When next they have to take in hand
The levies under their command
    In distant provinces.

Then deem it not an idle boast
That not alone from coast to coast
We soon may jeer at any host
    That may attempt invasion,
But give the lie to him who dares
To hint that aught as yet impairs
Our influence in the world's affairs,—
    Our honour as a nation!

THE AUTUMN OF 1872.

(A Fragment.)

Come, list to my new verse
About the Manœuvres,
You really might do worse
 Than lend me your ear,
Till I sing you how MICHEL
Left Blandford and Critchell,
And battles fought which will
 In history appear.

Due northward his course lay,
Where WALPOLE in force lay,
" Take prisoners or slay
 Your foes to a man,"—

This he said with a smile, he
Then marched on the Wiley;
"Bang" went the guns, while the
First battle began.

*   *   *   *   *

NOTE.—This being all that can be found, it would appear that the bard did not stay to see any more, "*relictâ non bene parmulâ.*"

A CAPTAIN'S PLEA.

WHO calls the soldier a machine?—
The two are most unlike, I ween,
    For instance, proud I feel, Sir,
When, after movement *bien fait*,
In barracks on Inspection-day,
I can regard my men and say,
    "*Not one spoke in that wheel, Sir!*"

THE ORDERLY OFFICER'S REPORT.

SIR,

I have the honour, as Captain of the day,
To send you of my duties the following *résumé*.
I visited the bread and meat at 7.5 A.M.,
And finding both were wholesome I resolved
    to pass the same ;
Precisely at 11 I the new guard did inspect,
And march'd them off : I'm glad to say I found
    them all correct ;
I visited the Hospital : the patients, to a man,
Said "no complaints," the wards themselves
    were truly spick and span ;
I then went round the dinners, the men I certify
When ask'd about their rations gave a *rational*
    reply.

At roll-call and at tattoo too reports I took, and these
Names mention'd in the margin were reported absentees.
From visits paid by day and night I safely may assert
The guard and sentries at their posts were sober and alert ;
I further certify that naught unusual did occur
During my tour of duty.

      I've the honour to be,

          Sir.

WAR LYRICS.

A.D. 1870.

"TO ARMS!"

Oh! that those bright heroic days,
Now living but in minstrel lays,
    Might dawn on us again!
When Glory's sleep should ended be,
And shades of ancient knights should see
Their long-forgotten Chivalry
    Resume her lofty reign.

Enter the lists once more, ye knights,
Ye who to breast a thousand fights
    Have urged your panting steeds;
Now gird ye quickly for the fray,
And bear ye well in the *mêlée*,
Though love be not the prize to-day,
    Yet bright eyes watch your deeds.

Time was when not a soul would hear
A summons to his heart so dear
 And linger heedless by;—
When on her knight each gentle maid
Would bind the scarf her hands had made,
And at the word would every blade
 Forth from the scabbard fly.

But now our Country hears the cries
For succour from our late allies
 In apathy and scorn;
While Honour bids us to the fight,
E'en Prudence calls us to unite
For right against the Despot's might,
 For treaties rudely torn.

GOOD TASTE (?)

FRANCE dies amid her wasted lands
    And homesteads in a blaze ;
" Spare not," the Battle fiend commands,
    And Germany obeys ;
While England stands with folded hands,
    And whistles the Marseillaise !

Oh ! if with peace we've grown obese,
    And blindly dream it pays
Like cowards to accept release
    From bonds of nobler days,—
For very shame's sake let us cease
    To whistle the Marseillaise !

E

AN AWKWARD AGE.

When little pets, in pantalettes,
   Just entering on their teens,
In eager way the world survey
   And wonder what it means;
Or when young rakes play ducks and drakes
   With land and heritage,
And lack, in sooth, their wisdom tooth,
   They're at—an awkward age.

When knaves succeed by fraud and greed,
   And telegrams tell lies,
When baby-farms cause vague alarms,
   And ironclads capsize;
When statesmen sleep o'er pitfalls deep,
   While Havoc's War-dogs rage,
You'll say with me, I think, that we
   Live in—an awkward age.

"*THE TIMES*" SURRENDER.

"We might almost say that, except for the reductions of the last year or two, our position would have been satisfactory at the present moment."—*Vide* "*Times*" leader, Sept. 26, 1870.

FROM disregard of precedents
   Popedoms and empires end,
And to the logic of events
   E'en *Thunderers* must bend.

So, in large type and place of state,
   We read this last *peccavi*,
Owning 'twas wrong to decimate
   Our Army and our Navy.

Brave troops their flags have had to strike
   Beneath Alsatian limes;
But where have ranks e'er wavered like
   The columns of *The Times?*

We gainsay not the will of Ζεύς,
    We take him at his word;
The Thunderer hoists a flag of truce,
    And yields his vanquished sword.

"TO RIFLE, ROB, AND PLUNDER!"

Two sorts of riflemen the War
    Parades before us neuters:
The Franc-tireurs free-shooters are,
    Their foes are all freebooters.

Oh! that fair France should wasted be
    To feed the German swine,—
This Schinderhannes' progeny,
    These Robbers of the Rhine!

THORWALDSEN'S LION.

(A Sonnet.)

SCOOPED from the solid cliff,
Within a stone's-throw of Lucerne's fair water,
With a majestic art that aye shall live,
Thorwaldsen has immortalized the slaughter
Of those devoted Swiss who fell for France,
Defending the untarnished *fleur de lys;*
The noble effigy
Might, were it possible, be deemed to show
An added torture in its sculptured woe;
For though no hostile lance
Pierces its heart, once more it guards the flag,
Draggled and torn like a mere tattered rag,
Compelled by neutral duty's stern decree
To be its gaoler in captivity.

NOTE.—This refers to General Bourbaki's army, captured and disarmed in Switzerland.

GERMAN RESOLVE.

'Tis fit the world should understand
    Count Bismarck's *Entschliessung*,
All shall belong to Fatherland,
    Who speak their *mother*-tongue.

HARK, BISMARCK!

No terms can e'er be entertained
    Involving occupation;
The veriest schoolboy knows the end
    Of terms is a—*Vacation*.

LUTETIA;

December, 1870.

'Tis *meet* your *meat* should *meted* be,
    Fair city of the fashions,
Since *cats* you *cater* eagerly,
    Nor *rats shun* in your *rations*.

"MILITIA EST POTIOR."

HOR., *Lib.* i. *Sat.* i.

I.

WHILE sitting in my study
With a batch of books from Mudie,
And indulging in a quiet little nap, nap, nap,
I had barely taken for-
ty winks, when at the door
Came a gentle little rap a tap, a tap, tap, tap.

II.

Ere I a word could utter,
Into the room there flutter
Three—what a painter cherubim would call, call, call.
I offered each a chair,
But they said " No, thank you, sare,
Besides, we haven't got the wherewithal, all, all."

III.

Then they say, "We're England's guardian angels, whom the bard
Saw sitting up aloft to watch poor Jack, Jack, Jack;
And we've come to flap the ears
Of your doting Ministers,
And make them steer on quite another tack, tack, tack.

IV.

"There are stirring times at hand,
And your rulers we command
To embody the MILITIA at once, once, once.
For that soldiers will be *nil*
Unless they've time to drill
Must surely be apparent to a dunce, dunce, dunce.

V.

"*Militia est potior*,"
Says Horace, and so boshy are

The plans that some empyrics would propose,
> pose, pose,
> That it makes us angels, weep
> While watch and ward we keep.
To see the nation led so by the nose, nose, nose.

VI.

Then straight away they flew,
> And gradually I knew
The visionary nature of their chat, chat, chat ;
> For the tapping at the door
> Had been really nothing more
Than the tail of Ponto dreaming on the mat,
> mat, mat.

ABSIT OMEN!

THERE was an old party called BULL,
Whose coffers were weighty and full,
    But to aid their defence,
    He'd not shell out his pence,
Nor give to his purse-strings one pull.

This was all very well, till one day
He was docking some items of pay,
    When a huge foreign force
    Came pounce on his shores
And took all BULL'S treasures away!

MISCELLANEA.

"I'M A SHOT."

I'M a shot, I'm a shot, I'm my Company's pride,
The range is my home, and my rifle's my bride;
Up, up with the flag, let it wave o'er the plain,
I've hit the bull's-eye, and I'll hit it again.

I fear not the sergeant, I heed not the cells,
I've a ball in my pouch on the target that tells,
And ne'er as a slave, but a soldier, I'll kneel,
With a most inconvenient seat on my heel.
      I'm a shot, &c.

VALENTINE.

The glad Spring comes, but not to me
    Its influence sweet imparting.
E'en now, with effort I repress
    The bitter tears from starting.

The zephyr's breath seems icy cold,
    The day appears benighted,
To the sad heart of one who loves—
    Whose love is unrequited.

Oh! surely man was never born
    Such anguish to inherit,—
To feel his heart weighed down with scorn,
    And not a hope to cheer it.

For sterner joys naught cares the soul
    When love's soft fetters fold it.
One smile from thee were worth the whole,
    Then, dearest, why withhold it?

"AND" & "ET."

On construing I take my stand,—
    If wrong, correct me, pray ;
You change your climate with your land,
    But not your mind, they say ;
Thus England has its gross gourm-*and*,
    The French their nice gourm-*et*.

CLUB LAW.

When Uncle Ned had no wool on his head,
    No Club would admit him—but why ?
Simply because the old gentleman was
    Black-bald to begin with. Oh, fie !

VERDI-GRIS(E).

A COMPOSER and a singer—the last must lose
  an eye—
Both one and other, in their time, of great
  celebrity.
(Imperial Cæsar o'er again!) If you their names
  should join,
They'll serve to show the rust which eats into a
  copper coin.

A VACATION COUPLET.

WHERE should a baker spend his holiday?
I ask, and Echo answers—*Alum Bay.*

ACROSTICS FOR POSTAL CARDS.

LET   us calm each worldly feeling ;—
ME   it pleaseth, when the crowd
PRESS   beneath the Minster ceiling,
MY   poor voice to raise aloud,
LIPS   of thankfulness to sever
TO   high Heaven, while we cry,
"THINE   our hearts are now and ever,
LOVE   and bless us, or we die."

I   cannot love you if I would ;
LOVE   such as mine, not understood,
YOU   would not prize, nor might we know
SWEET   interchange of joy and woe,
WITH   that affection, tried and proved,
MY   soul would seek in one it loved.
WHOLE   undivided love for me,
HEART   linked to heart by truest sympathy!

SYMPATHY.

'Tis night; the waves run mountains high,
   And drench the toiling crew;
I think of home, I heave a sigh,
   The vessel—she heaves *to!*

BY AN OLD FOGEY.

" *Quantum mutatus ab illo!* "
I say each night to my pillow.
   " *Illo* " here means
   A boy in his teens,
In turn-down collars and velveteens,
What a curly-haired darling I used to be!
   But now, you're aware,
   I've grown through my hair,
   And my face is furrowed with lines of care,
And each peeper is like a boiled gooseberry.

AN ILLUSION.

If those in search of a supper
   Will scan the shop windows with care,
And an appetite fit for a trooper,
   They'll find the following fare:
In Fleet-street—*Partridge and Cooper;*
   In Oxford-street—*Burton and Hare!*

CHARADE (*Honey-moon*).

My *first* on the palate may pall,
And the beams of my *second* may fall
   So coldly as true hearts to sever;
But my *whole*, dearest Loo,
If I share it with you,
   Will shed its warm influence ever.

CHARADE (*Wo-man*).

My *first* is what my *second* gets
  When he my *total's* slave is!
The exception to the rule is, let's
  Confess, a *rara avis*.

ECHOES.

When want stalks unheeded, what fiend shuts
  your eye?
In accents reproachful comes Echo's reply,
  " Luxur-*y*, luxur-*y*."

What means are the best, then, to open your
  eye?
Back comes the refrain on the wings of a sigh,
  " Penur-*y*, Penur-*y*."

DEFINITION.

Pray, what is a widow?
A women that's rid o'
   Her husband, and puts on a cap.
And what is a widower?
One that is rid o' *her*—
   Sometimes a fortunate chap.

A DISTINCTION WITH A DIFFERENCE.

The Laureate speaks of "airy navies
   Grappling in the central blue;"
      'Tis true—
This may be *in futuro*.
But, in our own days, hairy navvies,
   Grappling on the village green,
      I've seen,
And that not far from Truro.

BY AN OLD BACHELOR.

When to my arms a parent gives
A babe she deems the best that lives—
　　A little fright, it may be,—
Compelled to say a word of praise,
I murmur, as I fondly gaze,
"Well, I've seen many in my days,
　　But this one IS—a baby!"

THE TWO VOICES.

She. "I am monarch of all I survey,"
　　When I look in the glass I can say;
　　Then why such a treasure divine
　　To the hands of another resign?

He. But to give and receive is our duty,
　　So if love you obtain for your beauty,
　　See yourself in these eyes, and still say,
　　"I am monarch of all I survey."

A RATIONAL INFERENCE.

Now if "*amantium iræ amoris integratio*,"
Then surely, *nihil pertinet quodcunque ego facio;*
For as a bill returned with costs by Nathan Moss renewed is,
So a free pardon till next time the upshot of our feud is.
Then think not Justice Hannen will e'er our lives dissever,
For when we've fought we'll kiss again, just as good friends as ever.

"TWO OF A TRADE, &c."

Ye hard-worked tailors and hardy sailors,
    Why don't ye better agree, men?—
'Twixt cutlass and goose there is little to choose,
    For ye both are equally *seam-men*.

MIND v. MATTER.

I.

"*Æquam memento,*" quoth the bard
Of Tivoli, "*rebus in ard-
    uis servare mentem.*"
If hardness and ill-fortune try
Your mind's fair level to destroy,
    Says he, you must prevent 'em.

II.

But now, when ice and snow combine
To overthrow these legs of mine,
    I can't be so particular
About the level of my mind;
Sufficient is the task, I find,
    To keep my perpendicular.

LAND AND WATER.

Who, in the days of axe and brand,
Invaded once the Holy Land,
To wrest it from the Paynim's hand;
    We praise those gallant raiders.
But equal honour they must have,—
Our sturdy oarsmen, staunch and brave,—
Who urge the lifeboat o'er the wave,
    For they, too, are *crews-aiders*.

PAT *v.* SAMBO.

If a powerful term you choose to employ,
You'll call your friend Paddy a *"broth of a boy;"*
    But he's quite cut out by the other:
For Sambo or Quash, or whatever's his name,
Can establish a far superior claim,
    For he's both a " *man* and a broth-*er !* "

MORAL CRABS.

MANY " live that each to-morrow
  Finds them farther than to-day ;"
But, as they confess with sorrow,
  Farther *back*. *C'est bien vrai*.

FROM ENSIGN BLANK, OF THE —TH.

SWEET are the tints that autumn sheds
On leaves that fall about our heads
  When seated in the grove ;
But rosier hued, and sweeter far,
Autumnal " leaves of absence" are
  To subalterns in love.

JANUARY 11TH.

Hilary Term!
There is surely a germ
Of a sly sort of satire here to be seen.
How grimly ironical,
"*Lucus a non*"-ical!
Hilarity's rare among suitors, I ween.

FORTUNA FORTES ADJUVAT.

He lives to fight another day
Who left his friends and ran :
Yet, since he "saved his bacon," they
Owned him the *rasher* man.

TO VOCALISTS.

If you to a lady went,
 Humbly asking her to play
To your song accompaniment,
 This is what you ought to say—

No circumlocution—ah! no—
 Bow, and murmur what you want:
" Will you me *accompiano?* "
 Compound, brief, and elegant.

REFLECTION AT THE AMPHITHEATRE.

"*Nos salutant morituri.*"
Death's next victim may be you or I.

ANOTHER LIBEL.

Since ribston pippin
Caught Eve trippin',
All evils which have come to pass
Lie at the door of womankind.
This bitter truth is well defined
When mourners cry, "*A lass! A lass!*"

A NATION OF STATESMEN.

The key to our success behold!
If wallowing in heaps of gold,
Or living on the rates, men
Here feed on self-complacency.
So, bound in bonds of bunkum, we
Are all *United States-men!*

LINES TO A WELSHER.

Litera scripta manet—
A fact you are prone to forget;
   When the race is won,
   From the stand come down,
And cheerfully pay up your bet.

SEASONABLE PASTIME.

'MID a teazing wheezing we sing,
   Making unexpected rests,
Sneezing we our pleasing glee sing,
   Heedless of disgusted guests!

DEFINITION.

Now what is a matron ?—
A wife out of date run,
But buxom and fond of a beau;
While Paterfamilias
Oft is a silly ass,
Letting her carry on so.

FOREWARNED IS FOREARMED.

Should you be ask'd by some ill-manner'd bear,
Who in their talk seek witlings to entangle,
Why is a prison quarrel like a square ?—
The answer is—'cause each is a *quad-wrangle.*

A SUGGESTION.

Oh! Charley and Herbert,*
If Loyalty's curb hurt,
Your remedy's not far to seek;
Send a couple of pence
To your con-sti-tu-ents,
Say that each renegade his allegiance repents,
Which he sware to the Monarch each coin represents,
And I'll warrant you free in a week.

ON PARADE.

The word of command most readily obey'd is,
"*Officers fall out, and entertain the ladies.*"

---

* Sir C——s D——e, and Hon. A. H——t.

FROM THE SEALING-WAX OFFICE.

JUDGED by the test employ'd of yore,
  Condemn'd I fear I'll be,
I play the Scribe from ten till four,
  And then the Pharisee (the fair I see).
    (These lines are from a dandy clerk,
    Who in the season does his park.)

PHONETIC READING FROM OVID.

Habet ina castra Cupido—
Have a bet on the Chester Cup—I do.

EPIGRAM.

All singers have one fault, at least
    All those that I have seen;
Unasked, they never will desist,
    When asked, they'll ne'er begin.

CHARADE (Surf-ace).

When through my *first* they went aground,
Within my *next* of being drown'd
    Were all the hapless crew;
While o'er my *total* near and far
Floated sail, cargo, mast, and spar,
    So fierce the tempest blew.

THE RULE OF THREE—IN VERSE.

I.

The problem to be tried is
    Word-factors to arrange;
A sample see of my dis-
    covery so strange,—
As Vanity to Pride is,
    So Spite is to—*Revenge.*

II.

You say a wall is falling,
    And ask what's to be done?
The crisis is appalling,
    I answer—*prop or shun* (Proportion)

HARK!

What is the gambler's Paradise?
Echo responds,—a pair-o'-dice.

DEFINITION.

WHAT is a spinster?—
One who's evinced her
   Contempt for the masculine sex.
And what is a bachelor?
Student of latch-key law;
   Really his comfort is "x."

FROM THE CANTEEN.

IF of the soldier's liquor-money
   The *rationale* you would hear,—
You've named it. 'Tis his *ration ale,*—
   In other words, his dinner beer.

BY MY HAIRDRESSER.

He benefits his kind, I know,
    And adds to Nature's store,
Who makes two blades of grass to grow
    Where one did grow before;
But greater genius out-and-out
    That artist should be call'd,
Who causes crops of hair to sprout
    On heads that once were bald.

"'TWIXT CUP AND LIP.

In dewy meads there's many a slip,
'Twixt butter-*cup* and sweet cows-*lip*.

Q. E. D

YOU ask what instrument's the best
 To play " Adeste Fideles " ?
I say, if *sound* be any test,
 Doubtless *a dusty fiddle is.*

MR. L——E, (from Australia,) *re* THE INCOME TAX.

IF the world has five quarters, why should not
 the year, too ?—
Though I'm told it the public bewilders ;
That the globe *has* a fifth is a fact I can swear
 to,
And so can my friend, Mr. C———s !

A SONG OF THREE AND SIXPENCE.

"*Do me, do me,*" says the Dome of Saint Paul's,
    But little our visitors know,
How terribly they'll get done as well,
    If up to that Dome they go.

THE NEW SPEAKER.

THE 'cuteness of the rapier, and the temper of the foil,
The keenness of the scimitar to cut the Gordian toil,
The strength that trusty broadsword or claymore gives the hand,
May these be all united in our newly-chosen BRAND.

THE LOVE-SICK WINDOW.

CHLOE her lattice loves to fill—
  Where suburbs end in lanes—
With mignonette and daffodil,
  And woodbine, which she trains.
Ah! well—like me, her *window's-ill*
  Looks green and full of *panes*.

AT CHURCH.

WHEN a well-known extortioner we view,
Sleek and demure within his cushion'd pew;
'Tis then we may the proverb understand—
Many a clean glove hides a dirty hand.

CHARADE (*Pun-gent*).

My *first's* a breach of social laws,
   My *next's* the snob who did it,
My *whole* the avenging mustard was,
   Which seized his tongue and bit it.

A HEALTH TO THE PRIMATE.

Long may the union 'twixt Church and Tait,
Remain unsever'd by the hand of fate!

IMPECUNIOUS.

What time my purse of cash is bare,
   Such caution it engenders,
I don't go too far East, for there
   I'm sure to meet *Mi-le-nders*.

SONG OF THE SEATED.
(1869).

I'M a member, I'm a member,
    Though my foes did prophesy,
When return'd in last December,
    I'd be out before July.
Then the voters, then the voters,
    Were bribed as bribed could be,
But luckily, my bloaters,
    It wasn't done by me.
              I'm a member, &c.

I was merry, I was merry,
    When the Judge revising came,
And in no sort of a hurry
    Upset their little game.
Now I'm seated, now I'm seated,
    Beyond the reach of ills,
The petition is defeated—
    Hurrah for Justice WILLES!
              I'm a member, &c.

A NEW VERSE.

Join in the chor-i-us,
Whig as well Tory as,
Would she were more wi' us,
God Save the Queen!

CHARADE (Stud-iou's).

At Cambridge I my *first* did sport,
(Newmarket's handy, very,)
My *next* are the results it wrought,
Quæ longum numerare;
If I my *total* more had been,
I should not now be short of tin!

HOOD MODERNIZED.

Take her up tenderly, lift her with care—
None knows how dearly she paid for her hair!

VALENTINE.

'TWAS when the light of the stars was quench'd
    By Aurora's brighter ray,
And the tiny flowers had just begun
    Their delicate tints to display,
That Nature rose from her mossy bed,
And with anxious haste to her storehouse sped.

A spacious cave of adamant
    Received the Parent-Queen,
When hark! a loud resounding cry,—
'Twas one of sorrow, not of joy,—
    Burst from the realms unseen.
Her fears were true, for, sad to say,
Many a charm had been filch'd away.

Now, would you know what Nature miss'd
    From her goodly store of charms:
Then hearken; there lack'd two beautiful feet
    And a pair of rounded arms:
Nor were these all, for had they been,
Her sorrow had been less, I ween.

But a graceful neck, and auburn hair,
And hands as alabaster fair,
    They, too, alas! were gone;
And a pair of dark and sparkling eyes,
Such as the Faëry Queen might prize
    To gaze on Oberon;
And a mouth she had moulded not long ago,
Shaped after the model of Cupid's bow.

    (*Chorus, after Æschylus:*)

Now judge if Nature had right to complain
Of the many years she had toil'd in vain,
And think how happy the mortal must be
Who possesses the fruits of this burglary.

She summon'd Cupid, hovering near,
　　That lover of frolic and mirth,
And she bade him string his golden bow
　　And speedily fly to earth :
If haply he might have luck to find
The stolen beauties among mankind.

Cupid, delighted, outstretch'd his wings
　　To seek the stolen spoil,
But, it must be own'd, did not expect,
　　In the search to have much toil ;
For the urchin knew full well that she
Who possess'd the charms must unrivalled be.

Many a palace he hurried by,
Though many a beauty might in them lie,
And straight to a well-known spot did fly,
　　All else behind him leaving ;
Ambrosial odours filled the air,
For lovely Thisbe found he there,
Entwining lilies in her hair,
　　And myrtle garlands weaving ;

A lovely rosebud she, scarce blown,
Ah! well might Cupid proudly own,
That ne'er before such beauty shone—
    He quite forgot the thieving!

Of all the maids, on whom angels' eyes
Have ever gazed from the starry skies.
    She was the *Prima Donna.*
And the charge she found 'twas vain to deny,
For she was the culprit most evidently,
    The goods being found upon her!

CHARADE.

HERE'S a charade on "*off-ice*," consider'd rather fine,
Composed by men on duty at the frozen Serpentine:

 Our *total* is our *last* to watch,
  And keep the folks my *first*,
 Or fish them out with due despatch,
  If they should get immersed.

WHY, INDEED?

THE bird that pours its captive strains
 Is rightly called canāry;
The loft, then, which your corn contains,
 Why is it not granāry?

CONFESSIONS.

When young in years and strange to vice,
    I pined for pretty faces,
Then rosy cheeks and big round eyes,
    Form'd of my dreams the basis.

In after years, when more mature,
    I scann'd the darlings' figures,
And all complexions could endure,
    So they fell short of niggers.

But now, grown philosophical,
    I con both forms and features,
Nor less, though ne'er in love I fall,
    Adore I the dear creatures.

Since dark, and fair, and stout, and thin,
    I equally desire all,
They laugh and call me a marine,
A land and water go-between,
    A General Admīr-al!

A FRAGMENT.

I HALTED in my walk, and stood at gaze,
One of a multitude who stay'd to stare
At a long line of mourning carriages
And hearse with carven panels rich and rare.
Its four black horses with their nodding plumes,
Guarded by mutes and by attendant grooms,
Long-tail'd and sleek, had fatten'd well on woe,
With manes as dusk as "Manes" from below,
Thus rolls, methought, the tide of Life along,
Another wave breaks on the eternal shore!
This, haply, was a man renown'd in song,
Whose name his country heard but to adore;
Or was it one of England's golden youth,
Whom Fate forbids his fortune to enjoy,
Tiger-like, tearing with untimely tooth
Life, wealth, and titles from the hapless boy?

And seeking knowledge, as my custom is,
I ask'd a mute "Whose funeral is this?"
In pompous tones that functionary said,
With scarce a bend of his sepulchral head,
"*The Allied Funeral Companies, Limited!*"

THE TOWER, OCT. 17TH, 1871.

AN ACROSTIC.

B ENEATH the gloomy fortress which he ruled,
U nder such shrine our hero fitly sleeps;
R esting like him in whose wars he was school'd—
G reat Bonaparte—near the river's deeps.
O h! noble heart, when aiding in their flight
Y oung Prince and Empress o'er the stormy sea,
N ever did chivalry own fairer knight!
E ngland may well weep long for loss of such as he.

RHYME FOR "SILVER."

For "Silver" a rhyme
Was made in no time
    By this 'coon:
Take nitrate of silver,
And you will be ill ver-
    -y soon.

A FRUITFUL THEME.

When Paris gave to Venus
    The prize of the most fair,
Say, Muse, which fruit in causing
    Troy's woes had largest share?
Was it his golden apple,
    Or Sparta's *gilty pear?*

A PLEA FOR THE GARDENS.

I AM not quite a reprobate—
    Still less am I a greenhorn,—
And yet, I think, to close its gate
    Is rather hard on Crēmorne.

Though haply boyhood's days are o'er,
    Past freaks were sweet to dream on ;
Old faces met you by the score
    Beneath the lamps at Crēmorne.

What other spot the palm could win
    For sweet *meringues* with cream on,—
For fowl and lobster salad, in
    The supper-room in Crēmorne?

And 'tis the truth that, in my youth,
    Full often did I see Morn—
With guiltless eyes—light up the skies,
    While driving home from Crēmorne.

ON SEEING THE DESIGN FOR THE NEW LAW COURTS.

'Twere long to tell all we miss
In frowning o'er this page,
The plan a patchwork dream is:
Relent, ye statesmen sage,
Make not our Courts of Themis
The mis-take of the age.

EPIGRAM.

Matilda can't from Jane exist asunder,
This is a thing which must perforce bewilder,
'Tis only equalled by another wonder,
Which is—how Jane can tolerate Matilda!

EPIGRAM.

The world is full of fools, and if
You'd ne'er behold an ass,
All by yourself you'll have to live
And—*break your looking-glass!*

RECIPE BY A POETICAL CHARWOMAN.

If you should paint your sleeve, there ain't
Nothing so fine as turpentine;
Water's no good, not though you should
Go down and drain the Serpentine.

TO MY DENTIST.

I ALWAYS think my Dentist would
If mounted, prove a rider good;
For he is daily wont to show
His skill with screws in *rotten-row!*

THE FORTY-SECOND.

OUR regiments in fight or storm
    True fortitude discover;
But *one* is in such splendid form,
    (We met them once at Dover),
That when they don their uniform
    They're *forty-two'd* all over!

INTERCEPTED POSTAL CARDS.

Supposed by the writers to be quite unintelligible.

(The italics are mine.)

No. 1.

May and June have charms of their own,
I mutter aloud, when the wintry winds
Come and pierce me through muscle and bone,
To button my "Ulster" it me reminds.
"*See*," I say, as I reach my home,
"*You* blinding sleet, you're in dreadful form,
To-night I leave you to those who roam,
Love to be hardy and breast the storm."

No. 2.   The Reply.

"*Come*, shopman," I cry, "your tariff's too high;
At thirteen and six I much better could buy,
Nine shillings are plenty for socks, such as they 're,—
Dear at the price, too, they'd be, I declare."

I, not finding this quite as good as a play,
Am bound to confess that, as neither gave way,
All rigidly firm as a couple of rocks,
Alone he was left to contemplate his socks.

HIGH CHURCH COUPLET.

IN spite of vetoes vague and mystic,
To Ritualistic ritual I stick.

AN ECLOGUE.

I.

Says Army to Navy,
As well be a slavey
As now hold commission, I ween;
Says Navy to Army,
Yes, truly her palmy
Days each sister service has seen.

II.

Says Army—*sans* purchase
We're left in the lurch as
Completely as toads in a hole;
Just think how 'twill vex one
To feel one's selection
Is under friend Cardwell's control.

III.

Says Navy—the worst is,
You can't count on justice,
Suppose a mishap to occur ;
    The swells must be shielded,
    So all that your zeal did
Vain sympathy only will stir.

IV.

Says Army—some millions
Of purblind civilians,
In peace-time don't scruple to say,
    From the duke to the drummer—
    Like chimneys in summer,—
Soldiers are but a useless display.

V.

Says Navy to Army—
I vow it would charm me
To have a good rattling war ;
    Says Army to Navy—
    My boy, *I belave ye,*
And they both liquored up at the bar.

A FRAGMENT.

High on a rock, o'er the deep valley frowning,
    Rearing its head o'er the mountains afar,
Seeming but part of the crag it was crowning,
    Stood the proud fortress of Graf Uam Var.
        None but a chosen few
        Path to its portals knew,
Hewn out of granite from apex to base;
        Such the stern fastness where,
        Couch'd in his tiger's lair,
Slumber'd grim Ulric, the last of his race.

Slumber'd, indeed, but, with restless upheavings,
    Labour'd his breast like a storm-ridden sea,
Naught could the thought of his famous achievings
    Lay the fell demon none witness'd but he!

Sons he had rear'd and taught
'Gainst him, their Sire, had fought,
Red from their slaughter his broadsword he
sees ;
Priest, serf, and seneschal,
Vassal and henchman tall,
Wait but his last breath his castle to seize.

* * * * * * *

SPRING.

Who's this fair maid, all the landscape adorning,
    Sweet is her beauteous form to behold,
Her face, lightly tinged with the bloom of the morning,
    Shineth with lustre far brighter than gold.
        Flaxen her tresses flow
        Over a neck of snow,
Soft as the down on the butterfly's wing,
        'Neath her arch'd eyebrows too
        Gleam her soft eyes of blue ;
Name we the maiden ;—'Tis beautiful Spring !

Ah ! now we name her, a thousand will claim her,
    One they have sigh'd for for many a day,
Hearts that once wild were, and since have grown tamer,
    Bound as in childhood beneath her glad sway ;

But to the young she seems,
Gilding their boyish dreams,
Pledge of a cloudless hereafter to bring,
" Rapture like this," they say,
" Never can fade away,
Ours is an endlessly beautiful Spring!"

Haste then to meet her, with open arms greet her,
Hers are the buds, and the blossoming leaves,
Arrogant Summer in fruits may defeat her,
And Autumn triumphantly point to his sheaves,
But when the wintry blast,
Frosty and chill, is past,
Earth's hundred voices will joyfully sing,
" Chief of the seasons four,
Welcome as heretofore,
Welcome, thrice welcome, most beautiful Spring!"

FRIENDSHIP.

LET those who never felt its spell
    Refuse to join our chorus ;
But some there are who know full well
    The magic word before us.

Say, schoolboy, say, what charms to-day,
    And gilds the approaching morrow,—
What angel finger points the way,
    And soothes scholastic sorrow ;

That with the touch of sympathy
    Speeds on the flagging hours :
'Tis gentle Friendship standeth by
    And strews thy path with flowers.

And is that name forgotten when
    The world's clouds darken o'er us,
When boyhood's years their flight have ta'en,
    Which naught can now restore us?

No! then 'tis sweet some heart to meet,
    And its soft influence own,
That bids you prove a brother's love
    Nor seek to mourn alone.

No one is so accurst by Fate,
    So utterly forsaken,
But some one, if he bring a plate,
    Will give him beans and bacon.

So, as at first I said we would,
    Cheer loudly, near and far—
And take the time from me, my good
    Friends—hip, hip, hip—hurrah!

EXODUS.

(For translation into Latin Hexameters.—100 lines.)

Oh! sacred Muse, that, with the touch of Truth
Inspired the Sage to sing the birth and youth
Of God's Creation, and to draw the veil
That first enshrouded the unrivall'd tale,
That told of our first parents' hapless crime,
Fraught with result of woe to endless time.
Thou, that with heavenly breath didst keep alive
The flame that glow'd within his volumes five,
Pardon the wild presumption that would dare
To reproduce a page so rich, so rare,
As that which speaks in words well worth their fame,
Of the great time when out of bondage came
God's people Israel; and if there remain
One spark of fire to flash athwart the brain,
Grant it to him who, trusting, undismay'd,
In humble faith thus seeks thy potent aid.

The heart is harden'd still of Egypt's king,
And God's successive plagues have fail'd to bring
Home to his breast repentance, for his throne
Is not more marble than that heart of stone.
From when the cry first from the land uprose,
Where writhed the Chosen in oppression's throes,
And ere the Shepherd of Jehovah's choice
Had seen the burning bush, and heard the voice
That spoke the purpose of the Eternal Mind,
To mark him in its wisdom from mankind,
And by his means to lead the Chosen Band
To their inheritance, the Promised Land;
Through all this time hath Pharaoh's wrath burn'd high
Against the victims of his tyranny.
The serpent-rod, the rivers turn'd to blood,
The cattle struck with murrain where they stood,
The hail and fire, smiting herb and tree,
The darkness, horrid both to feel and see,

The locusts, breathing terror and dismay,
And blighting hopes of harvest in a day,
On his proud heart these judgments fall in vain,
Still tighter round his slaves he draws the chain.
Yet think not, Pharaoh, that the Lord of All,
At whose dread nod thrones totter, kingdoms fall,
Will 'bate one tittle of His word divine
For opposition impotent as thine,
Nor dare to cope with Him who reigns above,
When He demands the children of His love.
E'en now the Almighty wings the avenging dart,
Which, when all else has fail'd, must reach thy heart.

'Tis midnight,—and on Egypt's burning plains
And mighty cities sleep celestial reigns;
Sleep, the unvalued, priceless gift to man,
Nightly descending since the world began.

But on this fatal night the air is stirr'd
With breezes strange, and suddenly is heard
The rustle of the Death-Angel's sad wings,
Filling the soul with dread imaginings;
He, the Death-Angel, girt with awful power,
And sent from Heaven in that accursèd hour,
When man's first crime, pregnant with ills immense,
Call'd forth the anger of Omnipotence.
Not now he comes to give the weary peace,
To tottering age to bring a glad release,
To those who long the loved and lost to see,
Or from his chains to set the captive free ;
What now his errand, what his purpose fell,
Let the wild cry of Egypt's daughters tell,
Who, with a grief not to be thought or said,
Woke from their sleep to find their first-born—dead !
Here lay the guiltless babe, new-born, and there
The stalwart youth, with frame to do and dare ;

No house escaped, from his who till'd the ground
To his who sway'd the sceptre, throned and crown'd.
But not unmoved *he* saw his own blood flow
To swell the fearful catalogue of woe,
And forced at last to bow beneath the rod,
He own'd the matchless power of Israel's God.
Triumphant was their exit from the land ;
For with an outstretch'd arm and mighty hand
He brought them forth, rich with their captors' spoils,
Elate with freedom, from their recent toils.
How shall I sing the wisdom and the grace
With which Jehovah led His Chosen Race!
The wondrous power that curb'd the vaunting boast
Of impious Pharaoh, when, with mighty host,
With hate renew'd and unrelenting hand
He sought to crush that Heaven-protected band;
Attempt how fruitless!—For the obedient sea
Parted its waves that Israel might be free,

Dry-shod they cross'd old Ocean's sandy bed,
For on each side the billows backward fled,
While the Great God, who fought on Israel's side,
Whelm'd the Egyptians in the refluent tide.
And Israel saw the wonder from afar,
Horses and chariots and the men of war,
With Pharaoh's self, unworthy of his throne,
Discomfited, engulf'd, and overthrown.
And all again was still. The waves once more
Closed on the ruin that they shrouded o'er,
But through the silence rose the chant of praise
To Him whom e'en the troubled sea obeys,
And with one voice they bless'd the Lord of All,
Who on that day brought Israel out of thrall.

www.ingramcontent.com/pod-product-compliance
Lightning Source LLC
Chambersburg PA
CBHW022138160426
43197CB00009B/1335